D0100996

*True Basics of Real Success
through natural philosophy*

BEFORE THE BEGINNING IS A THOUGHT

True Basics of Real Success
through natural philosophy

Written by Phil Murray

Illustrated by Ginger Gilmour

First published by

PeRFECT WORDS and MUSIC Limited

1994

Copyright © 1994 Phil Murray

Illustrations Copyright © 1994 Ginger Gilmour

PAC of CARDS Copyright © 1994
Allison Murray
Ginger Gilmour
Phil Murray

No reproduction without permission

All rights reserved

British Library Cataloguing-in-Publication
Data available

ISBN 1-898716-10-2

Printed in Great Britain by Elite Printing Services, East Grinstead.

This Book is Dedicated to
the PAC

*Our business in the Universe is not to deny its existence,
but to LIVE, using the Laws to rise from lower to higher ...*

*We are all on the Path, and the road leads upward ever,
with frequent resting places.*

The Kybalion Hermetic Philosophy

Contents

What Why and When

The path of Personal Development is as long as you wish. Half way along that length another Path can be seen. This route will take you all the distance that you would have travelled had you remained on the path of Personal Development, and then further.

Some stay on the first path and flourish. Others stay on the first path, flourish, and wonder what it is like on the other Path they can see running parallel to the one on which they travel. Some cross over too soon on to the other way and are not prepared for the nature of this route less well travelled.

Others follow my golden rule of *Gradual Graduation*.

I believe in Personal Development.

I believe in the encouragement of *Private Victory*.

I also believe that this type of victory can atrophy ... unless transformed into *Public Victory*.

Ultimate Victory is **Service.**

to begin with ...

You are a special person!
I ask that during the reading of this book, and at all other times, you treat yourself as such! There is no one in this world quite like you, and to that degree you are in fact unique. The ideas that you are able to create in your mind, perhaps had external stimuli, but you are the catalyst that mixes these idea generators with liberal portions of your own distinctive brand of thought, to create something new for this World.

Fascinating isn't it!

The more you understand This Physical World, Universal Intelligence, Your Body, Your Mind ... and YOU the GNOSTIC BEING, the greater will be your contribution to life, and resultant pleasure.

The Seasons are not clearly defined and radically differ as you travel around the Planet. I know of nothing else as tangible and natural as these indistinct time periods, with which to align one's own outlook ... both metaphorically speaking ... and absolutely. I know that those of you not experiencing the Seasons as I have described them, will understand that this writing is as poetic as it is factual.

Life comprises many rhythms and vibrations. The pendulum can swing from one extreme to the other, and I know of no person able to defy this natural law. I do know of those able to enjoy the positive swing, who then rise above the negative which often follows ... the pendulum still returns, but they are above its influence and able to maintain their onward progress.

You are about to contemplate, begin, or continue, on a Path leading to ever increasing amounts of awareness. With perception and awareness comes power, and the knowledge of the correct usage of this force does not necessarily accompany it. Stay in shallow water until your swimming is strong ... then find the oceans and swim with the sharks ... as a dolphin.

Should I ask if you enjoyed gnoating, you could not tell me, as gnoating is not part of your vocabulary. You would be unable to conjure up a picture of this pastime I call gnoating. This means that gnoating would be one avocation unavailable to you consciously. Behind every word is an idea. The more words you understand, the greater amount of ideas you will be capable of enjoying. Your mental lexicon is a direct contributor to your accomplishment ability in all its forms. You must add to it routinely!

If I asked you to gnoat with me, and you placed your arms around my waist ready to dance, I could laugh or be offended. If I was shy I may avoid you in the future. If I lacked decorum I might engage verbiage in an effort to return the offence. You see gnoating does not have any connection whatsoever with dancing. You would have a misunderstanding of the word gnoat, and thus the action of gnoating.

If you doubt your understanding of any word then consult its definition in a good dictionary. The most important tools with which you must equip yourself for your new future are the very best dictionary that money can buy, stimulating books and aware people. The derivation of a word can be particularly useful to your understanding of grander concepts, and all good dictionaries will show these etymologies. The greater your vocabulary, the easier your passage to success through natural philosophy will be.

For the record, there was no such word as gnoating, so I have invented both it, and its meaning. I define it as follows: Gnoating ... the act of passing a word that you do not understand without referring to a dictionary and clearing the meaning of the word fully with yourself. *Slang*: dullard; illiterate; dolt; person lacking brightness.

Don't be a gnoat ... get a dictionary!

Now I invite you to Before the Beginning.

If the concepts are real and practical to you, then you have full liberty to enjoy the rewards that any increase in awareness will help float your way.

I implore you to explore the possibilities of Altruism and Philanthropy with open heart and wise being.

The solid, old era of Pisces is almost completely behind us, and we are at the dawning of The New Age of Aquarius. Exciting and fresh prospects await this new development for Mankind on Earth.

We have a duty to examine the unimaginable, and place the slights and sneers of a thousand cynics firmly to one side, lest they cloud our vision and impair our enjoyment of the New Age which is now upon us.

Previously unimaginable levels of personal and inter-personal achievements are available to an ever increasing number of people. The ways in which we go about reaching out for this success will play an important part in the future outlook for the Planet as a whole.

The era of, "grab and run," is passé.

The age of, "win at all costs," was embarrassing.

The fashion of, "who cares as long as we are all right," never did work out really.

New ideas involve internal effort to facilitate absorption and utilisation of the benefits and service that they entail.

If you are happy with the World as it stands ... with the old ways of looking at problems ... patriotism and traditional values ... ! If you think that God is on your side and not the other ... that your secular religion is more relevant than your neighbour's .... and people matter most as long as they do not get in your way ... !

If you feel that any of the above traits belong to you and you are not willing to change them for the better, then Before the Beginning is not for you, and may I suggest if you are browsing through it in a bookstore, that you replace it on the shelf and choose another title?

We can part company friends!

H. P. Blavatsky reminded us of the fact that, *"There is no Religion higher than Truth,"* in her classic work entitled, *"The Secret Doctrine."* Whenever I am in a quandary I ponder those words and they seem to illuminate the answer to which I aspire.

The *Win For All* ingredient is readily available for the cessation of all conflicts around the Planet.

The greater understanding of fellow Mankind is possible through the increased use of telepathy. Hunger will cease when economics are viewed as an inferior concept ... tolerance will see an increase in popularity ... this will happen!

The New Era is with us and let me remind you ... while we are improving our abilities as Stewards over all we survey ... whilst we are bringing about an end to pain and suffering ... as we meditate and educate, enrich and enhance ... remember to enjoy life on this Planet as it is meant to be ...

Light ... Happy ... Soulful

May Peace and Happiness forever remain your Guardian Angels

Phil Murray

Winter ...

what does the future hold?

Planning the garden

*Let Light and Love and Power restore the Plan
on Earth ... from The Great Invocation*

I see a time in the not too distant future,
when the roles of work and play will be reversed.
I can visualise a working environment so enticing
to the ambition and goals of the average person,
play will be a distraction to the actual purpose of
that individual.

I have a vivid picture in my brain of happiness
and prosperity, giving and giving, achievement and
peace of mind, for every individual who is able to
embrace the viewpoint that honour, integrity, and
natural laws, are the most vital elements of true
success.

The limits of imagination are the only distractions to the realisation of this dream. The habits of today and yesterday that have got us this far in the game of life, are sadly no longer relevant to the furtherance of achievement, and that honourable goal of happiness for the human race.

In order to be happy, we must be engaged in an activity that is part of our *raison d'être*. We must be actively working on our purpose line, and showing ourselves to the World that we are worthy of life on this Planet.

I also see a future where rat eats rat ... where the fat rat gets fatter before the fat rat gets squashed by a slimmer rat aspiring to obesity. That future is geared towards short term targets, and a philosophy of fear related incentives which inspire only those of us who are so far down tone that we see no further than the fat rat.

In this environment, the artist is scoffed and the street wise uneducated kid of a thousand neighbourhoods rules the roost. So as he rules, so the culture deteriorates further into displays of personality, at the expense of exhibitions showing true character.

This society does not know authentic happiness, but it understands cruelty and is motivated away from it in order to achieve what it thinks is joy.

In this world of shrinking mores, the remaining members of society who have retained the ability to think and see things from new viewpoints, hide away, lest their sole remnant of civilised life be confiscated from them.

Two visions ... two possibilities!

So where do we go from here?

Society is as great as it has great thinkers. Thoughts are things, and the future tomorrow has been visualised in the present today. "The significant problems we face cannot be solved at the same level of thinking we were at when we created them," said *Albert Einstein*.

The gardens of today, were the thoughts of yesterday. If our thinkers are frustrated, or not adequately rewarded ... if they are tolerated but not encouraged ... if their true worth is gauged in volume rather than quality ... then that attitude will be reflected in a future of short term gain and long term loose.

You will work the soil for turnips, then plant roses and fully expect a good showing of both.

We have a chance to get it right!

There is a movement sweeping the industrial world that has focused on *Quality* as its tenet. It is that word *Quality*, which inspired one of the viewpoints that enabled this book to be written. *Quality* does not tolerate deceit, and no amount of psych up Band Aids, or motivational seminars will tempt *Quality* to give up its ideals in favour of the bribe.

The *Quality* movement sees a rosy future that needs to be created now, but is willing to sacrifice and wait, before reaping the rewards of those creative thoughts and visualisations.

True basics of real success are established in character. The only genuine and permanent success must deal with fundamental issues. To establish a successful character, you must examine your ability to deal with the principles of integrity and honesty, fairness, human dignity, service to others, quality and excellence, human potential, patience and tolerance.

If you build your character around these natural harbingers of success, then you may enhance the resultant characteristics with personality traits, as and when you wish. It cannot ever be the other way around. These laws of character and personality cannot be reversed if you are contemplating long term gain.

The smile is sweet if the person is happy.

We can all learn to smile, just as we can study the latest street jargon. We can school ourselves in contemporary platitudes and hammer home the current formulae for achieving targets. We can accomplish these tasks quickly ... the issues of character take longer to embrace and internalise.

You must learn the laws of the Physical Universe, and their mastery will bring you real success in this World, but a measure of your true achievement will be found in your ability to transfer your ambitions and desires into a higher plane of aspiration.

This book suggests that success based on natural philosophy, is the only real and lasting fulfilment that we should be aiming for; until that is, our new found ethical stance and mastery of natural law in this life, allows us access to a higher existence.

The Earthly guidelines offered here are inspired by the law of reap and sow. An examination of five years in the average garden would provide a similar philosophy, if the gardener was true to the land.

We have however, the real world to deal with. Small business and giant corporation. Individual and family. Deviant and conformist. Country and country. Accent v accent.

Where do we begin?

We start as we mean to finish!

Commence and continue with the conclusion you desire firmly to the forefront of your thought patterns.

Individual and Corporation alike. Small garden and giant landscape ... whichever.

We commence our task thinking about what we want in the end. The rose bush will have to be planted in good quality, fertile soil. The position for best results is full sun. Only if you plan your garden this way can you expect beautiful blooms throughout the season.

I see that future where individuals rule the world through interdependency. The beauty of one part of the garden, enhancing the strength of another. The weak and insipid colours in the borders, enjoyed as a contrast to the vigour of the brazen, gaudy insect attracters. Trees protecting shade loving plants, and allowing climbers to clamber all over them.

This natural philosophy has plants living side by side, sharing the soil ... taking out and putting back ... flowing with the organic qualities of the earth ... cyclical attitudes.

Where the striving for spiritual awareness is the goal, and life is the means of achieving that end, I see a time when honour will be honoured and peace will reign supreme. The furtherance of mankind as a whole will mean more than all the petty squabbles of ten thousand lifetimes.

I see that time.

That time is the era of the individual whose insight acknowledges the merits of a group. I have a bright mental image picture in my mind of that day when all Mankind pays homage to the past of a million philosophers, and then quickly gets on with the job in hand, eyes firmly on the present, then the future.

I see that time.

When we all postulate the future as a beautiful place; that is when this Haven will begin to materialise at a more rapid pace.

Thoughts are things.

Before each beginning is a thought!

Everything that you perceive now, began life as a thought. There are many different levels of existence. There is a chair ... a photograph of a chair ... a reproduction of the photograph of that chair ... someone's interpretation of that reproduction ... the original design drawing of that chair, the interpretation by the original craftsman ... but at the very beginning, someone conceived of the idea.

The very first thought about that chair was the beginnings of its materialistic form in the physical universe. The thought is merely another medium for expressing the senses. The thought is material. It is a different type of solidity to that which we can see through eyes ... but solid nevertheless.

We have made massive technological leaps forward into the future of what just a few years ago were thought of as wild dreams. I believe that the science fiction of today, is no more fiction than the science fiction and wild dreams were of yesterday. I see a future where fascination will change its course to embrace the wonder of the human mind.

I am an ontology student of the mind as a vehicle for the Being, and I invite you to join me. The relationship of the psyche to the mind to the brain to the body to the world ... it is a meditative passage of no return. You cannot have knowledge without taking responsibility for what you know, and once you embark on a journey of thought discovery, there is no turning back.

Once you are aware of the awe inspiring power of the human mind, there is no solace in harbouring unprincipled desire. Full responsibility comes when you are answerable to the world for the thoughts in your head, and so, first of all, let us think the right thoughts. Let us all embrace the idea that thoughts are things, then lo and behold, before long, you will see for yourself that this is so.

What you are is what you have been
Contemplating privately
Secret thoughts come straight to view
As your surroundings mirror you
The World is merely what goes on
Inside your own cerebrum

When you are cognisant of this simple fact; it is then that you will feel a need to change some of the workings of your mind. It is then that you will seek out help to change what seems to be incontestable. But just like anything that you are privileged to see in the physical world, whatever you wish to change begins with the thought that it has already changed.

What thoughts can you think to shape the future?

Will you join me in shaping a good future for everyone?

Will you decide right now to take steps towards recovering lost friendships and adopting new concepts?

Will you forgive the unforgivable?

Will you trust in yourself?

Will you believe, that whatever you believe will happen, will?

Will you take steps to re-shape your thinking?

Will you take full responsibility for yourself and others?

Can you embrace the character ethic?

Will you look through the personality traits to meet up with the real person?

Will you take time to learn a better philosophy, and then when you have learnt that one, study another?

Do you swear on oath of allegiance to the cause of beauty?

Have you decided to end fascination with distraction?

Are you strong enough to withstand an invitation to revisit old ways?

Are you brave enough to espouse new viewpoints?

Does your future include success for others?

Can you believe in an alien belief?

Will you start as you mean to finish?

Do you wish for another?
Can you hear a new sound?
Does your heartbeat quicken
with each new viewpoint found?
Can you have good feelings alone with the weak?
Do you see yourself worthy, avoiding things bleak?
Have you planned your future, removing
resistance?

Acknowledge your greatness
Inspire your existence!

Plan the garden exactly as you wish to see it in the seasons of many years to come ... then reward yourself by thinking the highest thought you can manifest in your head!

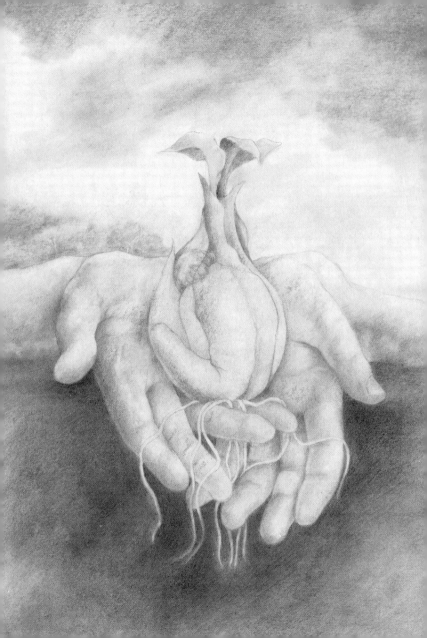

Spring ...

the talk comes alive!

Seeding the garden

Man ought to be ever striving to help the divine
evolution of *Ideas*, by becoming to the best of his
ability a *co-worker with nature* in the cyclical task
... H P Blavatsky *The Secret Doctrine*

It would be worrying to a den of thieves for
one of their number to suddenly declare himself
honest. It would be less worrying if that person
appeared increasingly virtuous as the years passed
by. With each display of integrity would arrive a
new convert. The gradient scale of acceptance
would slip into play.

"A person cannot do right in one department
whilst attempting to do wrong in another," said
Mohandas Gandhi.

We all have certain levels of wrongness both within us and around us. Some of us more than others. Accept the opposites that live within you. The good and the bad ... the love and the hate ... the fear and the courage ... the weak and the strong. None of these things are definite. There is no such thing as absolute.

At which point does coldness become heat?

Great power is there and available for those of you willing to hone the skills that will enable you to transmute the negative harmonics of any characteristics into their positive counterparts.

If you have made the resolution that your life ahead will embrace successful principles based around natural philosophy, then you must once again examine the garden. In the preceding season, we made plans for a garden we intend to enjoy in the future. We mentally planned it, and examined in the mind, our ability to embrace new viewpoints.

Can you grow a palm in the Arctic? Is it better to crop rotate? Do you really need a certain type of soil for success in your plot? Are you planning to flow with the natural qualities of your surroundings, or are you scheming to fight them?

In this season you will seed the garden.

It is not enough to plough the fields and

scatter. You must examine the soil to determine what might grow well. Ask all your neighbours what has worked for them in their similarly situated plots. Above all, you must know that as you plant a seed, a weed is making plans for its own survival!

Plant a seed, pluck a weed.

As the growth in your garden adapts to its environment by searching out light by every means possible ... so must you in your life. The ability that you enjoy, which enables you to adapt your environment to suit you is a privilege, should be viewed as such, and never misused capriciously. Adapt when necessary and change if need be, but use the power with great respect!

Whether or not your intention is to be a beacon and an example to us all, that is indeed exactly what you will become, as you strive to improve your life through the natural laws that surround you. Any departure from the norm will be viewed by most with disdain. Some will leave you, some will follow. Some will criticise, some will ask advice. Some will hate, some will love. Some will create and some will seek to destroy.

Having limited skill as a surgeon, you would not commit yourself to a life and death situation connected with the lungs of one patient, knowing that in the next bed lies a person whose life you can definitely save by using your specialist knowledge of liver transplanting.

It is better to concentrate on what you can accomplish, rather than on what may destroy you. Thus, there will be people whom you can go back to collect once the main assignment is accomplished. Do not endanger the mission for the sake of the cynic!

Constantly weed the garden!

Your new principle centred future will materialise at a rapid rate, but you must transmute all negative influence along the way to a more beneficial harmonic.

Negativity acts like a brake, and eventually as a reverse gear! When you positively take one step forward, negativity is the two steps back. You see a bright future of fairness and achievement through your positive paradigms; a colleague sees a future through his negative lens, and it is black!

Two mental maps ... two concepts of reality at variance with one another. Neither map is the actual territory; these charts are merely a perception of the region. Your map is optimistic and clear, his map is doleful and stained.

Your vision makes him nervous!

Weed as you seed!

Real success is a living example of itself. You must live the talk and characterise the philosophy. There will always be someone waiting in the wings, watching the performance in full fault finding mode. They seek the defects and deficiencies, the shortcomings and the weaknesses; thus establishing for themselves that success based on natural philosophy does not work. Our aim is not to prove them wrong through puerile altercations ... we want to lead by example. We live the talk, and that example becomes the beacon.

"What you are shouts so loudly in my ears, I cannot hear what you say," wrote *Ralph Waldo Emerson.*

Inculcate into your mind, that which you wish to become. Constantly impress yourself with the good characteristics of integrity, honour, friendship, service and interdependence. Trample into your beingness the concept of fairness and trustworthiness. However esoteric the art of inculcating yourself with these virtues may appear, you will discover over a period of time, that what you focus your thoughts upon, you will eventually become.

You are now placing into your life, the people whom you wish to grow and prosper alongside. You are planning life long relationships ... planting oak trees which will only be enjoyed in full, long after you have departed your present lifetime on this Earth.

"As a man thinketh in his heart so is he."

This aphorism is a workable tool which can help remind you of responsibility to yourself and the rest of the world. Whatever you internalise and truly believe in, is what you really are.

That is why I prescribe Affirmative Inculcations.

Tread into your inner self, that which you wish to become!

On the following page, I share with you some of my Personal Affirmative Inculcations.

Life is a game that I play so well
The power around me is mine to use wisely
Attracting the good is my own special bounty
I live to give and enjoy the reward
I live with the rules and transcend them
when need be
The honesty in me helps make me successful
I take all life's gifts and possess them completely
Harmony serenity joy and fulfilment
are always in mind when I contemplate taking
Strength is my strength and I relish my weakness
Love is my power and I share it freely
I love myself
I love Mankind
I love life

It is repetition of whatever you desire that will turn the matter of mind, into matter of a different vibration, which the human being can enjoy with full corporeal sensation. One may substitute *You* for *I*, and experience Inculcations as though they were being delivered to you from elsewhere.

Discover what works for you and develop the art. The use of aesthetic music is expeditious as it stimulates the right brain into an holistic understanding of what the left brain is accepting in a more logical and linear fashion.

I discuss Inculcations in a practical fashion under the heading of Positive Affirmations, in my earlier book entitled, *You Can Always Get What You Want*. The Cassette Tape of the same name has examples of my own Inculcations with music, using both first and second person pronouns. They also form part of the Cassette tape of this book. I utilise them, and approve their employment by you, as a practical tool which can serve you well.

The PAC of Cards at the end of this book will help form your own self designed future. Embracing the philosophies of forgiveness, strength, power and love, your prospects are elevated towards principles employed by the most charismatic and truly powerful people who have ever walked this Planet.

Employing the qualities of stillness and solitude, whilst contemplating your at-oneness with your surroundings and contribution to the Human Race, will allow a forceful level of mental concentration to emanate from you. Between stimulus and response, we have the ability to choose, and it is this mental quality that sets us apart from the animal kingdom. You are not your behaviour or your habits. You have merely added these idiosyncrasies to your pure beingness. You are unique in this world of living things as we know it, in having the ability to change your characteristics. You can do this by creating your own Affirmative Inculcations, brimming with high self esteem and total proactive capability, then living with them until they become connected to your beingness.

You must compose your own Inculcations!

You may like to affirm yourself with qualities that I have already mentioned. You may seek new characteristics for yourself, or endorse features with which you are presently happy and feel provide you with good service in life.

Integrity and honour, wholesomeness and truth. Trust and trustworthiness, initiative and decisiveness. Friendship, service and inter-dependence. Truth, brightness and awareness.

You have the ability to look at the way you think. This attribute may be lying dormant, but it nevertheless exists and sets you apart from other forms of life. It is your duty to use it by seeing negative mental actions as harmful, and changing these thoughts for improved ideas. Your life will become enriched, and the more you practice Affirmative Inculcations, the more enjoyable your new future will become. A positive impact from your new mental creations will reverberate around your circle of influence, and even the hardy old cynics, who exist in all walks of life, will begin to scrutinize their own lives for comparison.

The flower is watchable, pretty and glowing,
with attributes seen different ways.
Not always as bright or as full to each eye,
but forever is true to itself.
Learn from the Seasons and study this Earth
Inculcate all that is good
The Path may be steep but the trail
has been blazed
It waits for you patiently ...

The seeds that you plant in your garden now, are the flowers, fruits and vegetables that you will harvest at the appropriate time. Choose the seed carefully, remain true to your plan, and enjoy this season of the year to its full!

Summer ...

a steady course of action.

Watering the garden

Give a man a fish and you feed him for a day; teach him how to fish and you feed him for a lifetime ... *maxim*

You are about to embrace the philosophy of stewardship!

The concept of stewardship takes precedence over ownership. The theory of an interdependence capability is more easily adopted when you see yourself as caretaker rather than possessor of all that is yours. The sharing capacity of an individual increases when an ownership ethic is discarded in favour of the more workable stewardship concept.

There are seven separate energy levels of life

relevant to the work in this particular book, which I call the Strata.

I describe them thus:

Spiritus

Self

Family

Group

Mankind

Animal

Plant

A more enlightening illustration of the strata can be seen on the following page. The degree to which individuals can claim true success is in direct proportion to their strata interaction capability.

In each of the seven separate strata, exist many different energies. There are harmonics of life found on higher planes that can be experienced

on lower planes, but it is not until your Path has guided you upward that you will feel the full force of Higher Beingness. This postulate of mine is upheld by many other documentations, and I discuss it here briefly, only because it is through preserving the direction of your Path in the vanguard of your meditations, that real success will be forthcoming.

Let your mind dwell in the Stars, but keep your eyes on your feet, lest you stumble because of these ethereal contemplations!

Life is not about one aspect of its total. You are a Gestalt and the sum total of yourself cannot be reduced without loss of some quality. You have properties not derived from your constituent parts, and the combination of all your bits makes something else not available in any one of them.

It is this same Gestalt principle that produces magic formulae when like minded people with a single purpose get together in an effort to solve a problem. This is natural philosophy, and you are at liberty to take full advantage of it in your quest for honourable gain.

Success is having the ability to extract from the seven strata of life exactly what you want from them, without violating any rights in so doing.

You must ensure that you are asking the

49

relevant questions of life because you will get from it exactly what your mind dwells upon most.

You must plan for the future yet live in the present. Your planning is not just confined to Winter. It is a continuum which demands constant attention. Whilst enjoying your garden and its produce in the Summer, you may get sentimental for the future in the precise form you wish it to happen. Constantly honing the cutting edge of your mind, you enjoy what is in front of you whilst looking beyond.

In Winter, you planned your future. When Spring arrived you began to sow the seed of aspiration. This is Summer and you are learning and practising the art of Stewardship. That is looking after what you have created, with a caretaking eye on what others have also brought to bear in this wonderful world.

By staying true to your ideals of honour, integrity and winning for all, you will develop a personal magnetism. Just as sure as a sucker shoots from a rose, some of those attracted to you will have destructive aims in direct contradiction to your own direction. They are Human like us, but must be discarded with a kind word for the time being, in favour of the like minded force.

Watching over your ideas in action, you may

notice aspects of your endeavour that would be enhanced by a change of modus operandi. By all means change for the better, but not for the sake of variation. Stay true to your goals, and obtain your randomisation from elsewhere. You cannot keep pulling up a plant to see how its roots are progressing.

Summer is a time for watering the flourishing plants, and discarding the flora that failed to flourish, or perhaps did not look quite as you had expected when you planned and seeded.

Spread your time according to both pleasure and results. If you obtain enjoyment from pastimes that are less fruitful than others, then you must prognosticate potential outcomes and decide if you wish to remain active in those amusements. Not everything that you do in life need have intrinsic deep meaning as a pivotal ingredient. Frivolity lives to be enjoyed as a notion too, just as the gardener enjoys his Folly.

You may note moments of idleness during Summer, but it is only those of you who are inherently indolent that should fear any negative consequence. Life is not a dress rehearsal, and therefore should be ingested as it becomes available to you. The best time of your life is always the time that you are experiencing right now!

Continuously set aside three days for personal enlightenment … yesterday, today and tomorrow.

Health is a vital issue, and I address the body as an important component of true success. Ultimate gain is available only to those of you who practice gnosis. It is however, with great difficulty that the Being housed in an ailing body connects to a higher state. It is therefore sensible to challenge the body to do its utmost in a bid for excellent physical health.

You can live for months without food, and perhaps weeks without water.

How long can you exist without air?

Minutes!

Oxygen is the single most important element we must consider when meeting the challenge of corporeal well being. The Human body is a collection of interdependent cells, all relying on one another for life. The vital sustenance for all living cells is oxygen. Aerobic exercise is the motion which breathes this indispensable element into the cells, no matter how far they may be from the lungs. The first and foremost desire for exercise should be with this purpose in mind.

Disease in a cell means that the unit is literally not *at-ease* with some element of its existence. It ceases to be capable of an ability to respond. Its *response-ability* is lessened to the degree that it may die, or mutate, as in cancer. I suggest that disease is primarily caused by oxygen starvation, and is itself an attempt to cure.

We should interfere with this undertaking to heal from within as little as we dare. The body is intrinsically a self regulating entity, and it is my belief that in most cases, more damage is caused by the act of artificial cure, than the disease is capable of reeking itself.

Phlegm, spots, sores, aches and pains signal some of our bids to cure an ailing body, and we should not treat them as symptoms and strive to synthetically rid ourselves of the intrinsic cure. Rather, we must look at the disease itself, and put it *at-ease*. Unnatural habit patterns that we have allowed to invade our lives will be the most likely explanations, but oxygen starvation will be at the core of the problem.

Ensure that you exercise to oxygenate and not to build muscle at the expense of this crucial element. Anaerobic activity allows an oxygen debt, and the body literally ceases supplying this component of air to some areas, until a greater supply of it is more readily available. Be very sparing in your use of this method of exercise, and always use my rule of *Gradual Graduation* in whatever you do.

In the case of exercise ... *Show up* ... *Chin up* ... *Warm up* ... *Build up* ... *Speed up* ... *Keep up* ... *Lessen up* ... *Slow up* ... *Rest up*.

Every day in every way you must pledge to get better and better in everything that you do.

For your body, this means that you must treat it the way you wish it to facilitate you. If you let it deteriorate, then so will its service to you. Health problems arise as a direct consequence of abusing natural law.

The energy that you feed on must be compatible with your ability to absorb its nutrients. Potash is crucial for healthy tomatoes, but less necessary for sprouts and cabbage. There is no doubt about the fact that every human body has slight differences in requirements, but certain natural rules are universal.

Acid and alkali negate each other.

Certain foods need particular stomach juices for efficient digestion and absorption. You cannot mix comestibles craving an acid base for their successful assimilation, with those sanctioning an alkaline environment.

Your rule must be to partake of water rich foods as much as possible, and only eat one concentrated food per meal regardless. If you value the resources of our Planet, you should know that it takes ten joules of grain to produce one joule of beef, and twelve joules of grain to produce one joule of battery reared chicken.

You could just eat the grain.

If you wish to eat meat, remember that the taste and colour is derived from the waste product left in the putrefying muscle, which the animal was unable to excrete before death. You must therefore eliminate this waste through your own system.

Remember that meat is literally dead, decaying, rotting corpse, which is extremely difficult for your body's system to cope with. A high percentage of dead seventy year old men are found to have in excess of twelve pounds of undigested red meat in their stomach and intestines.

I propose to you through this natural philosophy of real success, that man essentially inhabits a body favouring a herbo-frugivorian diet. Fruit passes through the stomach and directly to the intestines, where it is absorbed within approximately twenty minutes, providing the stomach is empty and barrier free.

You are capable of living exclusively on fruit, and fruit alone.

The Innuit may disagree and should do!

It is for the individual to discover the most naturally harmonious eating patterns that best serve.

At the very least if it is possible, begin each day by eating fruit directly onto an empty stomach, and never eat it after anything else. Fruit will putrefy during its anticipation of digestion, if that lingering is too protracted.

The human body is equally comfortable with the contemplation and consumption of most vegetables.

This natural philosophy is as organic as the garden itself.

You need only observe what is effective without artificial stimulant, and practice it in your day to day regimen. You need both physical and mental nutrition, and I offer these carnal guidelines to support my belief that an uncontaminated, sound body, makes spiritual gain accessible to a wider audience.

Of course it is true also, that a polluted mind can destroy the body that gives it physical purpose.

You may witness a person's thought habits by their material manifestation in the body. A mind steered by evil purpose is a sign that the Being has relinquished control. You may view evidence of this in the eyes of the abdicator.

A lack of ontological presence is actually detectable.

We all have the choice as we ponder life's intersections, to choose good direction, evil bearings, or tracks in between these major highways. Enchantment with corruption will guide you to ultimate failure, just as sure as an alignment with natural philosophy will steer you to the fulfilment of your aspirations.

Before the beginning is a thought, and the absolute purpose of that contemplation is creation.

You may meditate on the swift climbers in your garden. They clamber all over your house, trees and outbuildings, and that is their entire purpose; to grow. You may also like to contemplate the less vigorous plant which allows itself years of caring cultivation, eventually from which it produces the most magnificent flowers, showing beauty and stroking at the heart strings of even the hardiest agnostic bigot.

I suggest to you, that true success takes time, and foundations must be as thorough as you wish the success to be. As a gardener prepares the soil, so must you cultivate your basics, and when Summer arrives, take some time to enjoy your creation before the busier season of Autumn.

I look around at my creation
wondrous of its splendour
Yet all it is and all it seems is me the
source and blender
I took the sun a pinch of soil some
water and a seed
I spent the time and nursed the ground
it gives me what I need
And yet it seems there is more to life
than what exists around me
A distant Plane vibrates and summons
All I am obeys the call
Happiness on Earth it seems
Is working towards Higher Means

Take responsibility for your creations and prepare for harvest!

Autumn ...

what the future held.

Harvesting the garden

So as ye sow, so shall ye reap ... *The Bible*

Give ... give ... give! ... then when you need to take, two gives still remain.

Autumn is a time for taking, and a chance to reflect on your achievements. You may enjoy your personal victory, as it is this private achievement that will allow you general success in the community at large for the following year.

You must be content with yourself before you can expect others to be cheerful with you. The law of the harvest states quite clearly that what you reap, is in exact proportion to the amount you have sown and effectively tended.

The wonder of natural resource will provide you with multiples from singles. One stalk of wheat will harbour many seeds. If this curiosity was not so, then neither would we be.

Remember during your meditation on success through natural philosophy, that weed begets weed. As it is in the field, so is it in the mind.

It is never any other way!

You must *act* before you can *accept,* and how you have *acted* will determine what you are now *accepting.* Why any Sentient Being should conclude denial of this natural fact is indeed a mystery of the Universe as great as Unending Space itself. If you are disappointed with the harvest, then it is actually a dissatisfaction with what you have sown and cultivated.

The sowing is the thinking and the reaping is the result!

Inspire, Perform then Receive!

That is the way it is.

You must develop principles that transcend what is demanded of you in the physical universe. This action will make rules obsolete. Choice is simple when performed from a sound mind steeped in integrity, and from this state, your internal direction finder guides you on a bearing for success.

Nostalgia is an obstacle to new ideas and personal development. Bigotry is a relative, and its adoption involves a stagnant attachment to tradition, which itself is a harmonic of symbolism; these traits often result in war.

I invite you to develop a nostalgia for the future!

Those of you allowing poor moral fibre to impinge on your spirituality will suffer the consequence of defeat after defeat, until you assemble your thoughts in a spiritually ethical and orderly manner, to reflect what you really want from life.

When you are deciding what to extract at the harvest, remember the goose that laid the golden egg continued laying. It wasn't until the greed of the owner propelled him to try and get all the eggs at once by killing the goose and searching for them inside the body, that he realised the goose was empty and the phenomenon had been cyclical.

Don't make that mistake. Recognise the merit of retaining some potatoes to begin the crop for the following year. As you spend the interest, the principle sum remains. If you merely spend some of the interest then the principle sum will increase, giving you more interest to harvest, and further ultimate financial joy.

If you are disappointed with the harvest, remember that you cannot ever cut apples from a briar, or roses from a thistle. The disappointment should be with yourself. It should not last for very long and you must quickly get into action a formula that will repel defeat and portend future glory.

You can have disease or be at-ease.

As you harbour negative thoughts, the wavelengths of this concern affect your body. You cannot escape this fact. You can pretend, and that pretence will be the foulest of them all.

The fooling of yourself!

This game that we all play in the physical universe is rigged in such a way that only those of you willing to transcend the animal habit can achieve true success.

I implore you to embrace the example of nature, but there is one model that is not mirrored in the garden, the animal kingdom or in fact anywhere else, except within you.

The wonder of Premier Imagination is available to you, and sets you apart from all other forms of life. Premier Imagination is your route to the Ether Waves, and it is here that the collective thought of all that has ever been contemplated in this World can be perceived. By using the Premier

Imagination through your Sub Conscious Mind, you may tune in and receive the answers to your prayers.

Faith and Determination are the two catalysers that will set your wish for the stars apart from any others. It is both of these ingredients that require focus and energy from your mind.

Mixing them with a clear and unequivocal desire for something very specific, is the mental equivalent of a physical explosion.

The same desire, living an elongated stretch of existence at the mercy of an unimpaired negative vibration, will surely make you fail just as much as Faith and Determination will force you to succeed.

Premier Imagination cannot be viewed in nature except as a result. To access these facilities you need only tell your Sub Conscious Mind what you require of it with a light thought, and then proceed with the physical act of accessing your desires, with Faith and Determination firmly in place.

The ethical stance of your modus operandi will affect your competence to play with this ability, and the depth of success you achieve, will be in direct proportion to your cleanliness of mind and purpose.

The tarnishing of your Beingness has been

wearing away at your abilities for lifetime after lifetime. It is with long term commitment only that you will achieve the energy necessary to begin the journey back to Nirvana. Before the beginning of this journey is the thought to make it.

The miscreant within you should be banished forever, and you must become a holy crusader to the cause of a perfect future.

Although the marvel of Premier Imagination is not tangible, its conclusions most definitely are. It is as natural as the tides and as available as air. You need but reach out and touch it with Faith, Determination and a light request. It will answer you with sweetness and be your saviour forever.

I write of these things in Autumn, as your harvest will have reflected your talent for co-operation with this inherent tool of good fortune. If you have reaped in plenty, then you may polish the scythe for the following year. If your acquisitions have been scant, you should check your intentions for honour! Preserve the scythe for the following year, which will be as productive as you are able to maintain integrity in your sphere of authority.

As you expand the quantity and quality of your knowledge, this new awareness will unveil a deeper experience of yourself. The more you know, the more you realise there is to know. Your quest for spiritual and material enlightenment demands a constant process of learning and expansion in your sphere of knowledge, and it will be apparent at your point of embarkation for this journey, that you may not break your voyage for any reason, without knowing that you have left the only true *Reason for Being*, behind you.

Winter is coming so celebrate life
I hope that you harvested gold
Another full year is behind you my friend
As we watch the future unfold
If you're feeling weary then rest up awhile
With feet up and log on the fire
Reward yourself fully and sing out a song
Your strength will return and your
life will be long
As sure as the seasons are true to the soil
Heaven is earth and there is joy in the toil
Forever again is the cause of true nature
As vast as deep glory with you the Creator
Before the beginning is always a thought
True basics can't lie and the truth can be taught
Real success waits for you arms open wide
Catch it embrace it we are on the same side ...

to end with ...

I am no Hierophant.

Perhaps like yourself, my status is neophyte. I understand the concepts of *totally cognisant* and *nothingness* being the same qualities, and am fully aware that it is to these states that I am presently aspiring.

I also believe in life ... I believe in people ... I believe in happiness and prosperity ... I believe in me ... I believe in you!

I believe that the Path of Transformation should be a celebration of rediscovery. I believe in nurturing the student and encouraging the misanthropic stray.

I believe in laughter.

I believe in the deep, the visible and invisible.

If I were expert in the postulates that I espouse, then more of my personal Path of Transformation would already have been travelled. My position as student of greater teachings is exactly that, and I am grateful if the writing of this concise volume is a help to you.

From my earlier book entitled, *"You Can Always Get What You Want,"* an organisation called the PAC has grown. We meet monthly in the modern workshop fashion, and enjoy an evening of varied viewpoints. There is also a monthly newsletter, and a book service for a wide assortment of titles.

PAC is an acronym for Positive Attitude Club. The PAC philosophy states simply that improvement of personal life through positive attitudes benefits Mankind as a whole. We are a non profit making organisation dedicated to peaceful interdependence and forward thinking for the World.

If after reading our Mission Statement, you would like to join us, then you are welcome.

I look forward to us meeting, and until that time, I extend my warmest thoughts to you for all aspects of your life.

Wishing You Happiness ...

Phil Murray

the PAC
Mission Statement
Through dissemination of quality spiritual and worldly material, living the talk and enjoying the Path of Transformation, we aim to render whatever assistance is required for The Journey.

Ultimate Goal
Premier State

the PAC *philosophy*
The improvement of personal life through positive attitudes, benefits Mankind as a whole.

the PAC *Visualisation Statement*

1. A large and increasing membership.
2. We aid members' awareness of positive reading, writing and viewing materials.
3. We help the world, with a constant output of positive affirmations from all members.
4. We influence the world for the better in every way, shape and form.
5. We show by example, that the PAC philosophy works.
6. We influence the Media, and World Governments, by living the talk of our philosophy.
7. We exist wherever there are people who can benefit and prosper from PAC Principles.
8. We are revered as an organisation of high principle, honour and integrity.
9. We aspire towards being consulted on any disagreements between peoples of the world, with the aim of solving all problems on a win for all basis.
10. Happiness during the Return Journey.

Phil Murray
Leader of the PAC *23 June 1994*

the PAC, Purbeck, Mill Lane, Felbridge, Surrey, RH19 2PE
Telephone 0342 322833

If you would like to join with us ...

The Positive Attitude Club accepts applications from anyone wishing to join.
All we ask is that you embrace the philosophy that anything
is possible with a POSITIVE ATTITUDE.

Name: ....

Address: ....

.... Post Code: ....

Telephone: ....

Occupation: ....

Contribution: ....

(towards monthly newsletter, meeting costs and general administration)

Let's enjoy today, and look forward to a rosy future ... together ...

Phil Murray
Leader of the PAC

PAC is an acronym for Positive Attitude Club
The PAC philosophy states simply that improvement of personal life
through positive attitudes benefits Mankind as a whole.
We are a non profit making organisation dedicated to peaceful
interdependence and forward thinking for the World

A Pac of Cards

Developed from an idea by Allison Murray

works like this ...

There are twenty eight different cards ...

four groups of seven.

Tear each one along its perforations until they are all detached from the book. They are smaller than regular credit cards, and can therefore easily be slipped into a wallet or purse ... weekly organiser or personal diary.

Use one per day!

At the end of each group of twenty eight days, shuffle the Pac and a fresh combination will be available to you.

Side one has a personal suggestion, and side two will show a similar sentiment in the second person, as if you are being told that message by someone else. Whatever you want to have happen must be accomplished in your mind first.

The altruistic and philanthropic meditations are the most powerful ... they can provide a person with an extra dimension to their personal thought patterns ... remember that Energy Will Follow Thought, and whatever you can hold in your beliefs as a Mind Fait Accompli, will eventually find a place in the Physical Universe, which is itself the mental creation in which we find ourselves operating ... most of the time ...

You must understand the power of this data and use it for the betterment of Mankind ... you cannot work for this honourable intent without being thoroughly successful yourself. That is how it works!

You must now illustrate this natural phenomenon with endeavour!

Meditate on each Affirmative Inculcation and then get into action! Lip service will not suffice ... you must believe ... belief is an intrinsic ingredient of the magic formula!

Have Faith and Believe!

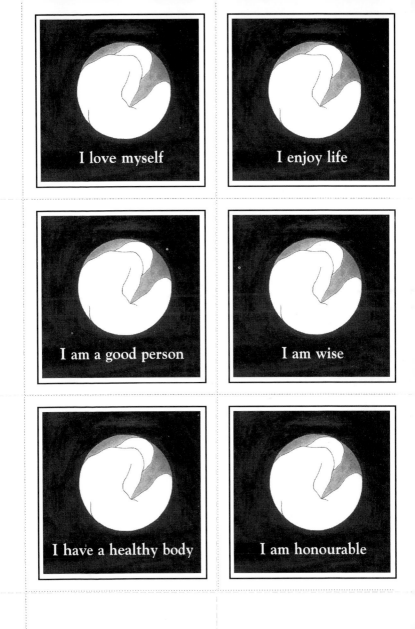

I am tolerant

I am a good learner

I am good hearted

I enjoy listening
to people

I am in control
of my life

I am powerful

My strength is
understanding

Love is my power

I love Mankind

Truth is my Guide

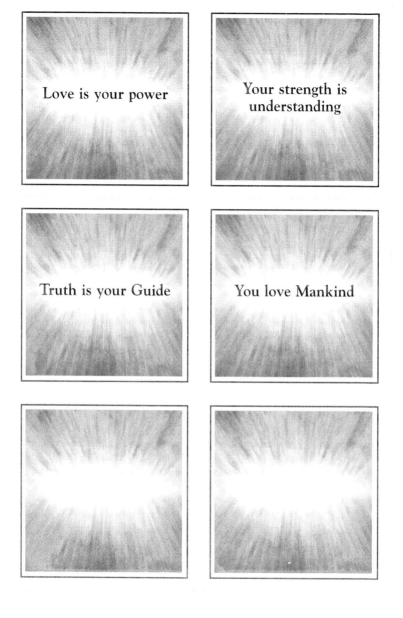

Further Stimulating Reading and Listening ...

*can be undertaken by obtaining the following books
and audio cassette tapes:*

Before the Beginning is a thought	Phil Murray *Book and cassette*
You Can Always Get What You Want	Phil Murray *Book and cassette*
As A Man Thinketh	James Allen *Book and cassette*
The Magic of Believing	Claude M Bristol *Book*
Jonathan Livingstone Seagull	Richard Bach *Book, cassette and video*
The Path of Transformation	Shakti Gawain *Book and cassette*
Man's Search for Meaning	Viktor E Frankl *Book*
The Three Candles of Little Veronica (for children)	Manfred Kyber *Book*
Trance-formations	John Grinder & Richard Bandler *Book*
Various works by	Alice A Bailey & H P Blavatsky *Books*
The Kybalion Hermetic Philosophy	Three Initiates *Book*
Memories	Nico Thelman *Cassette*

Some may be obtained from your local bookstore and all are available from the PAC

The Author

Phil Murray was born on the eighteenth of November 1953, in the North East of England. He was educated at Tynemouth Grammar School, before pursuing a career of writing, recording and acting in the entertainment industry.

In 1976 his interest and research into the subject of personal development began, but it was not until 1993 that his first book appeared in the bookstores.

His direct style is both popular and sincere.

His constant differentiations between character and personality; the respect he shows for the former and disdain for the latter, provided some of the stimuli which enabled this second book to be written.

The altruistic and philanthropic aspects of Phil Murray were cornerstones that helped form the Positive Attitude Club, which is better known as the PAC. This is a brand new concept for connecting the Force of Positive Thinkers throughout the World.

It was through the PAC, and Belgian Storyteller, Nico Thelman, that Phil met Ginger Gilmour. On their very first meeting it was agreed that Ginger should illustrate the book, with her own deep interpretation of life through art.

This book is also available as an audio cassette tape programme.

Make up your own PAC of Cards ...
and give exactly what you want to your life!

Who knows best how you really work?

You are the finest judge of what is right and wrong in your life. Design something positive for your future using a PAC of Cards as an aid to your mental prowess.

Imitate the Positive Attitude Club Cards idea using your own personalised sets of beliefs and self fulfilling prophecies. I wish you a peaceful and happy future ...

Visualising World Peace ... together ... with love

Phil Murray